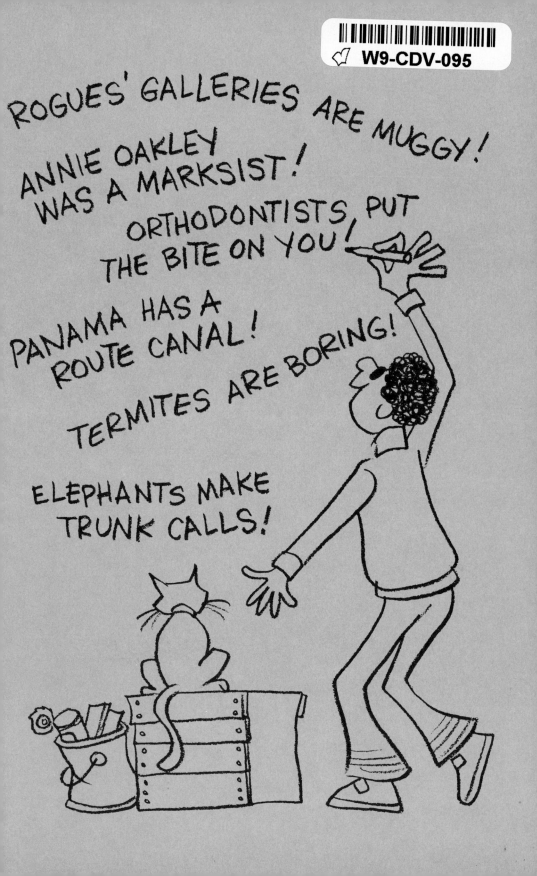

PINOCCHIO WAS NOSEY

Grandson of Puns, Gags, Quips and Riddles

Roy Doty

Doubleday & Company, Inc.

Garden City, New York

Other books in this series:

PUNS, GAGS, QUIPS AND RIDDLES
Q'S ARE WEIRD O'S
GUNGA YOUR DIN-DIN IS READY

ISBN: 0-385-12919-X Trade
0-385-12920-3 Prebound

Library of Congress Catalog Card Number 76-57873
Copyright © 1977 by Roy Doty

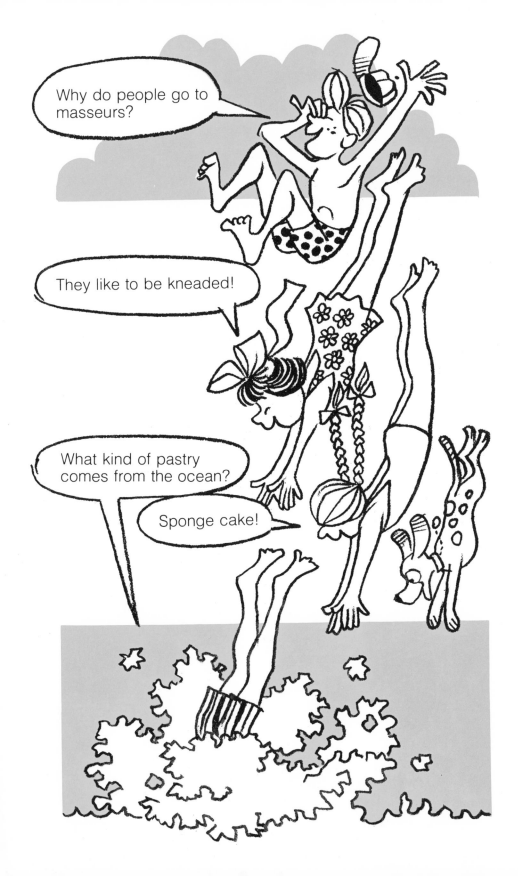

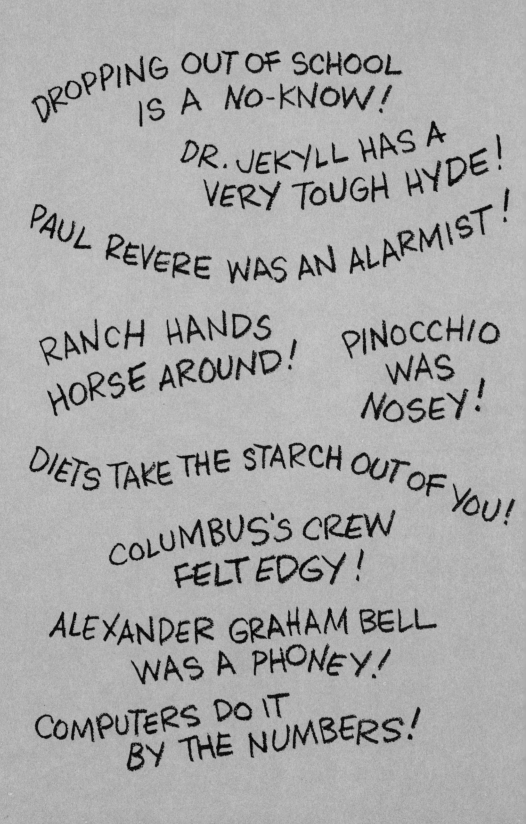